Plants
in Action

Library Edition Published 1990

Published by Marshall Cavendish Corporation
147 West Merrick Road
Freeport, Long Island
N.Y. 11520

Printed in Italy by New Interlitho, Milan

© Marshall Cavendish Limited 1989
© Cherrytree Press Limited 1988

Library Edition produced by DPM Services Limited

Library of Congress Cataloging-in-Publication Data

Kerrod, Robin.
    Plants in action / by Robin Kerrod: illustrated by Mike Atkinson
and Sarah Atkinson.
      p. cm. — (Secrets of science : 6)
    ''A Cherrytree book.''
    Includes index
    Summary: Science activities and experiments demonstrate how
plants make food and grow.
    1. Scientific activities — Juvenile literature. 2. Botany -
Experiments — Juvenile literature. [1. Plants — Experiments.
2.Botany -
Experiments. 3. Experiments.]
    I. Atkinson, Mike. [1]. II. Atkinson, Sarah, [1]. III. Title.
    IV. Series: Kerrod, Robin, Secrets of science : 6.
    QK52.6.K47 1989
    530' .078 — dc19   89-996
                                           CIP
                                           AC

ISBN 1-85435-157-5
ISBN 1-85435-151-6(set)

SECRETS OF SCIENCE

Plants in Action

Robin Kerrod

Illustrated by Mike Atkinson
and Sarah Atkinson

MARSHALL CAVENDISH
NEW YORK · LONDON · TORONTO · SYDNEY

Safety First

☐ Ask an adult for permission before you start any experiment, especially if you are using matches or anything hot, sharp, or poisonous.

☐ Don't wear good clothes. Wear old ones or an apron.

☐ If you work on a table, use an old one and protect it with paper or cardboard.

☐ Do water experiments in the sink, on the draining board, or outdoors.

☐ Strike matches away from your body, and make sure they are out before you throw them away.

☐ Make sure candles are standing securely.

☐ Wear oven gloves when handling anything hot.

☐ Be careful when cutting things. Always cut away from your body.

☐ Don't use tin cans with jagged edges. Use those with lids.

☐ Use only safe children's glue, glue sticks, or paste.

☐ **Never** taste chemicals, unless the book tells you to.

☐ Label all bottles and jars containing chemicals, and store them where young children can't get at them – and never in the family's food cupboard.

☐ Never use or play with electricity. It can KILL. Use a battery to create a current if needed.

☐ When you have finished an experiment, put your things away, clean up, and wash your hands.

Contents

Plants Alive!

Plants cannot move about, so they do not look very active. But they are active. We could not live without them. They provide us with food to eat and oxygen to breathe.

Most plants grow from seeds. Seeds do not look very special, but they are. They carry the complete plans for a new plant. See how many different kinds of seeds you can find. Don't just look in the garden. You'll find the best ones in the fruit and vegetables that you eat. Plant some and watch them grow.

bean flowers

bean plant

orange seeds

lemon seeds

apple seeds

corn-on-the-cob

wheat seeds

avocado seed

bean

peas

When seeds grow, they put down roots and send up shoots. When they grow in soil, you can only see the shoots. In this experiment, you can see the roots as well.

Grow a bean

1 You need some bean seeds, two jars, and some blotting paper.

2 Sow some beans in the jars. Place each bean between a roll of blotting paper and the glass, and put enough water in the jar to keep the blotting paper moist.

3 Look at the seeds every day. Soon, a white tip will appear from each bean and start to grow. Notice which way it grows – up or down?

4 It will grow down because it is a root. Wait until the roots are about half an inch long, and see what happens if you turn one of your jars upside down. The root will still try to grow downward.

5 Soon, a second shoot will grow. It will grow upward because it is a stem. Even if you turn the jar upside down, the shoot will grow upward.

bean pods

7

Water! Water!

Like us, plants need food and water to live. Sprinkle some cress seeds or some grass seed on a dry washcloth, and place it on a window sill. Sprinkle some more seeds on a wet washcloth, and place it next to the other one. Keep the second washcloth moist. After a few days, notice the difference between the two sets of seeds. The wet ones will have sprouted; the dry ones will be the same as before.

You can make interesting patterns or pictures with your seeds. Make an animal shape like the one below, or write your name.

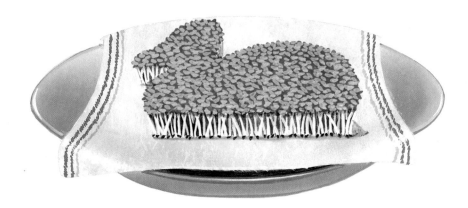

Plants drink water through their roots. Water in the soil passes through the root wall into the sap. The sap is a thick solution that contains the plant's food.

The water makes the sap solution weaker. Although water passes into the root, the sap does not pass out. This is because of a scientific process called **osmosis**. You can see how osmosis works with this experiment.

Pass the Potato

1 You need a potato and a peeler, some sugar, and some water.

2 Cut the end off the potato and scoop out a hollow in the flesh.

3 Stand the potato in a dish of water. (Slice off the round end so that it will stand up straight.)

4 Put two teaspoons of sugar in the hollow with a little water to make it dissolve.

5 Look at the potato a few hours later. You will see that the hollow is filling with water. The water in the bowl is passing through the walls of the potato by osmosis. It is trying to make the strong sugar solution weaker, like water in the sap.

Seeing the Light

Plants like to see the light! Fill two plant pots half full of moist soil, and sow some peas in them. Place the pots on the window sill, but cover one with cardboard so that no light can reach the soil. Water the plants regularly, and watch what happens.

The shoots in the uncovered pot will grow strong and green. The covered ones will stay pale and weak.

To grow well, plants must have sunlight. Therefore, they always grow toward the light. Plant some wheat seeds in a tray outdoors, and see how straight they grow.

Bring your seedlings indoors, and see how they all lean toward the window. Even if you turn them around, they will lean back again.

Cover the tips of the seedlings with little foil caps, and watch what happens. Then, see what happens if you trap a plant in a maze.

A-maze-ing!

1 You need a potato that is sprouting, a pot of soil, a shoe box, some cardboard, and some tape.

2 Tape cardboard "walls" inside the box, and cut a hole in one end of the box.

3 Plant a piece of sprouting potato in a pot at the other end, put on the lid, and leave the box in a light place.

4 After a few days, the potato shoot will poke out through the hole as it seeks the light.

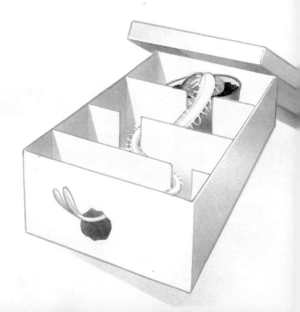

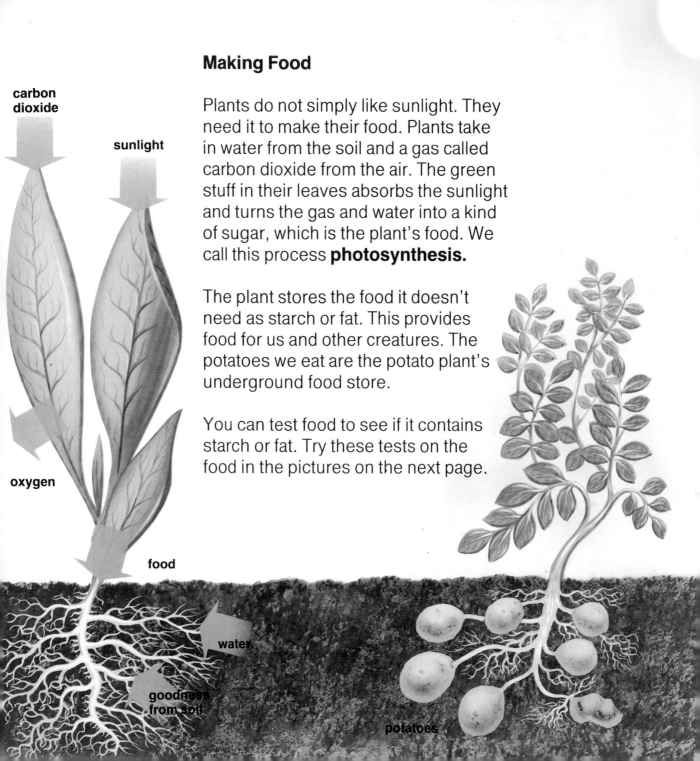

Making Food

Plants do not simply like sunlight. They need it to make their food. Plants take in water from the soil and a gas called carbon dioxide from the air. The green stuff in their leaves absorbs the sunlight and turns the gas and water into a kind of sugar, which is the plant's food. We call this process **photosynthesis.**

The plant stores the food it doesn't need as starch or fat. This provides food for us and other creatures. The potatoes we eat are the potato plant's underground food store.

You can test food to see if it contains starch or fat. Try these tests on the food in the pictures on the next page.

carbon dioxide

sunlight

oxygen

food

water

goodness from soil

potatoes

Starch Test

1 You need some iodine, some water, and a pipette or eye dropper.

2 Drip one drop of iodine on the cut food. Try a slice of potato first.

3 If the food contains starch, the iodine drop will turn dark blue.

Fat Test

1 You need some sheets of thin white paper.

2 Rub each food on the paper and hold the paper up to the light.

3 If the food contains a lot of fat, it will make the paper translucent – let the light through.

4 Try the Brazil nut first. Brazil nuts are so fatty that you can draw an invisible picture on the paper with one, and then make it visible by holding it up to the light.

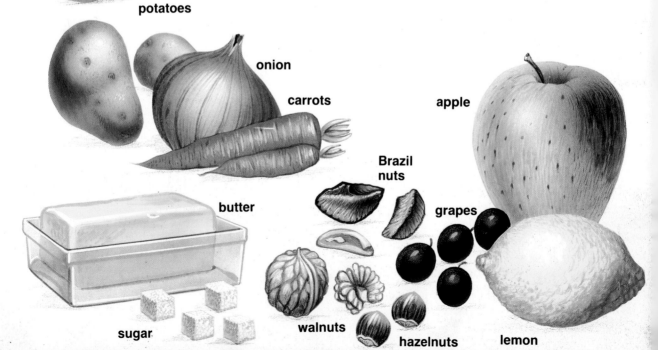

potatoes

onion

carrots

apple

Brazil nuts

butter

grapes

sugar

walnuts

hazelnuts

lemon

Bubble and Glow

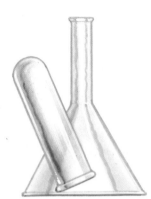

Have you noticed how underwater plants give off bubbles? They are bubbles of oxygen, the gas we must breathe to live. Plants give off oxygen during photosynthesis. If you have some aquatic plants, you can test for oxygen.

Oxygen Test

1 You need an aquatic plant, a bowl of water, a test tube, a funnel, a wooden splint, matches, and a friend.

2 Stand the bowl in strong sunlight, and soon you will see the gas bubbling from the leaves.

The gas will rise into the upturned tube and push out the water.

3 When the tube is nearly full, take it out of the bowl. First, let out the remaining water, and then trap the gas inside with your thumb.

4 Ask your friend to light the splint and blow it out. While the splint is still glowing, plunge it quickly into the tube.

5 The splint will burst into flame again. This shows that the tube contains oxygen, because oxygen enables things to burn.

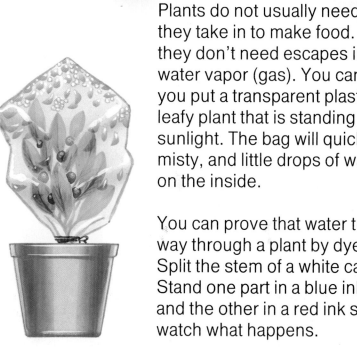

Plants do not usually need all the water they take in to make food. The water they don't need escapes into the air as water vapor (gas). You can see this if you put a transparent plastic bag over a leafy plant that is standing in strong sunlight. The bag will quickly become misty, and little drops of water will form on the inside.

You can prove that water travels all the way through a plant by dyeing flowers. Split the stem of a white carnation. Stand one part in a blue ink solution and the other in a red ink solution, and watch what happens.

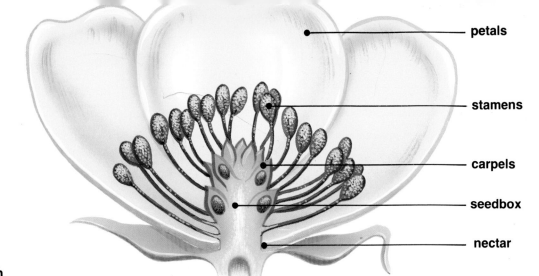

petals

stamens

carpels

seedbox

nectar

plantain flowers (pollen blown by wind)

Flower Power

Most plants grow flowers to produce seeds. Flowers have male parts and female parts. The stamens (male) produce a sticky dust called **pollen**. When pollen from one plant falls on the carpels (female) of another plant, seeds start to grow in the seedbox.

How does the pollen get from one flower to another? Well, some plants wait for the wind to blow it. Others rely on bees or other insects to carry it. They have bright petals and nectar. The bees come to drink the nectar. Pollen rubs off on their bodies, and they carry it to the next flower.

snapdragon flower (pollen carried by insects)

Make a Flower Press

1 You need two sheets of masonite, preferably with holes, two straps (old belts), some blotting paper and some old newspaper, and freshly picked flowers.

2 Put your flowers between two sheets of blotting paper, put newspaper on both sides, and then cover with the boards. Bind the boards tightly with the straps, and leave the press for a few weeks.

3 Remove the press very gently, and check that the flowers are dry. Then mount them on paper or card. You can make pretty bookmarks as gifts if you cover them with clear laminating plastic.

4 You could simply place your flowers between sheets of blotting paper, and leave them under a heavy pile of books. They will not dry out until later, after you have removed the books.

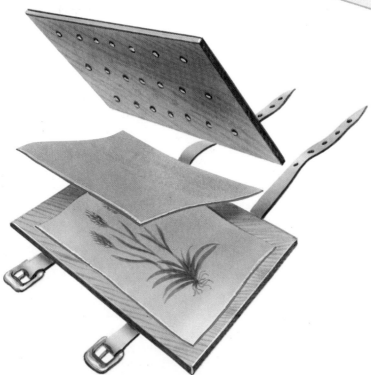

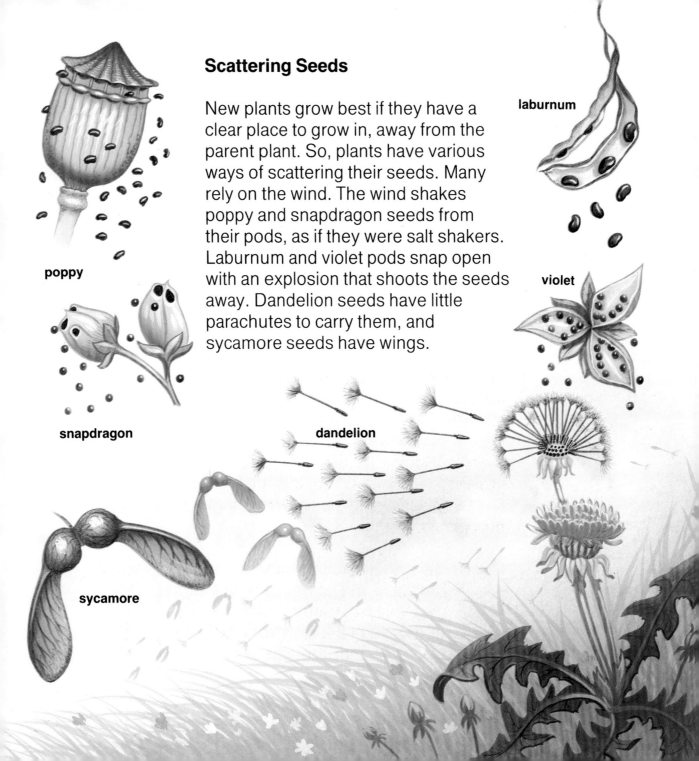

Scattering Seeds

New plants grow best if they have a clear place to grow in, away from the parent plant. So, plants have various ways of scattering their seeds. Many rely on the wind. The wind shakes poppy and snapdragon seeds from their pods, as if they were salt shakers. Laburnum and violet pods snap open with an explosion that shoots the seeds away. Dandelion seeds have little parachutes to carry them, and sycamore seeds have wings.

poppy

laburnum

violet

snapdragon

dandelion

sycamore

thrush

squirrel with acorn

mistletoe

Animals also help to carry seeds. The thrush eats mistletoe berries and wipes the seeds from its beak on the bark of a tree. The new mistletoe plant grows on the tree. Squirrels hide nuts in the ground to eat later. Often, they do not find them again, and the nuts grow into new plants.

Human beings also help to move seeds. Next time you go for a walk in a park or field, see what seeds you have transported. Scrape the mud from the bottom of your shoes into a seed box and see what grows.

19

Water and Weather

The biggest seeds of all are coconuts, and they are also the ones that travel farthest. Coconut palms often grow on sandy beaches. The nuts roll down to the sea and are carried away by the tide. They float on the waves until they are washed up on another shore.

Some plants like to keep their seeds away from water. Conifer seeds grow in cones. The cones release their seeds only when the weather is dry. Then, the wind can blow them away. So, you can always tell the weather from a cone. It will open when it is dry and close when it is wet.

Ferns make sure that the weather is good before they release their spores (seeds). Look at the back of fern fronds, and you will see rows of spore pods. Pick a fern frond and do this experiment.

Fair weather Frond

1 You need a fern frond, a magnifying glass, an eyedropper, a flashlight, and some clean white paper.

2 Remove one spore pod from the fern, and put it on a sheet of white paper.

3 Hold the magnifying glass over the pod and shine the flashlight through it. Watch the spore pod open and release its spores.

4 Now, drop a little water on the pod. Watch how quickly it closes. This action keeps the spores from being released in damp weather.

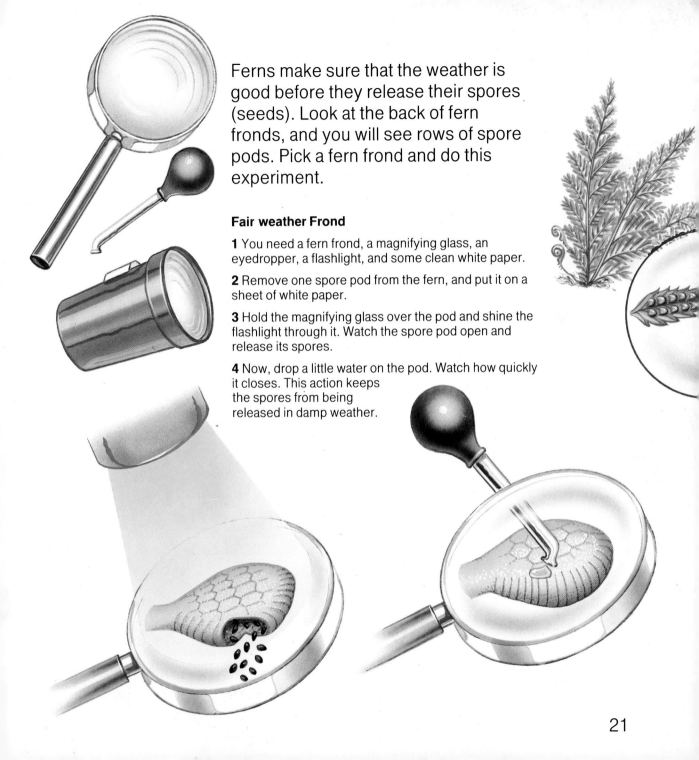

21

Spores Galore

Mushrooms are fungi. A fungus does not produce seeds. It has almost invisible spores. They grow on the dark gills under the cap. The best way to see them is to make a print of them. Use an open mushroom bought from a grocery store. Do not pick mushrooms you find growing. Some of them are poisonous.

Make a Spore Print

1 You need an open mushroom, a sheet of white paper, and a glass bowl big enough to cover the mushroom.

2 Carefully remove the mushroom's stalk. Place the cap, flat side down, on the paper. Cover it with the bowl, and leave it for a few days.

3 Carefully lift the bowl and the cap. You will find the pattern of spores on the paper. If you want to preserve your print, spray the print very gently with artist's fixative.

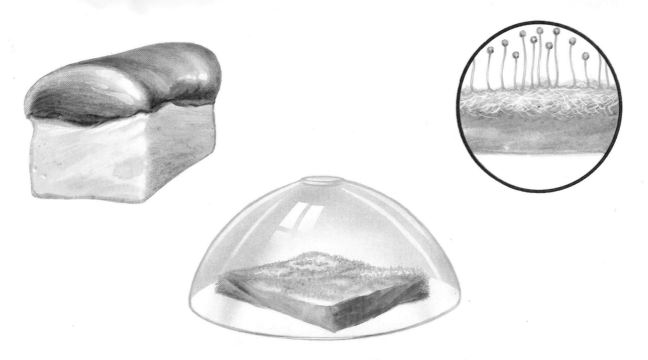

Unlike green plants, fungi cannot make their own food. They have to feed on other things, like fallen leaves in the forest. There are fungus spores in the air all around us. Some cause the mold that sometimes grows on leftover food.

Put some pieces of damp bread under a glass bowl, and see how quickly mold grows on it. The mold grows from invisible spores trapped under the glass. Try leaving some cheese, or lemon peel, or other food to grow mold. See how many different kinds of mold you can grow.

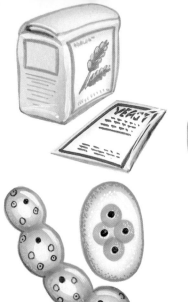

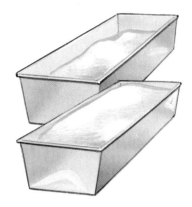

Raising the Dough

Yeast is a fungus that we use in cooking. It makes bread rise. The baker mixes yeast, flour, salt, and water and kneads it into a dough. Then, he leaves it for a certain period of time. The yeast feeds on the flour and gives off carbon dioxide gas. Bubbles of this gas get trapped in the dough and make it rise, or grow in size. This makes the bread light when it is baked.

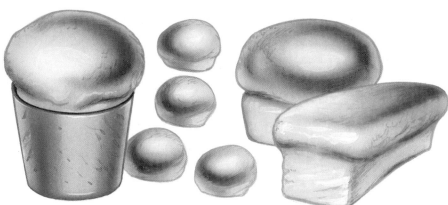

Get an adult to help you bake your own bread. There are lots of recipes in cookbooks and magazines for simple yeast bread. Shape your dough into rolls, or bake it in a loaf pan.

You can do an experiment to show that yeast gives off carbon dioxide.

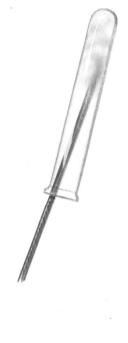

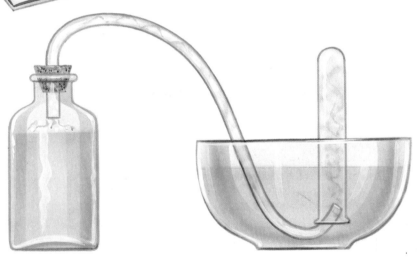

Testing for Carbon Dioxide

1 You need a bottle with a cork, a plastic tube, a test tube, a bowl, water, sugar, some dried beer-making yeast, matches, and a splint.

2 Make a sugar solution with 1½ cups of hot water and 3 teaspoons of sugar.

3 When it is lukewarm, pour it into the bottle and add a teaspoonful of yeast.

4 Shake the bottle and cork it. Make a hole through the cork and insert the tube.

5 Put the other end of the tube under water in a bowl and cover the end with a test tube.

6 You will soon see the yeast working as gas starts bubbling into the tube.

7 When the tube is full of gas, plunge a lighted splint into it.

8 The flame will go out. This shows that the gas is carbon dioxide, since carbon dioxide stops things from burning.

A Bottle of Bubbles

Practice your scientific skills and please your friends with this yeast experiment.

Soda Pop

1 You need two plastic buckets, several bottles with screw-on tops, a pitcher, a funnel, a piece of cheesecloth, weighing scales, and the following ingredients: cream of tartar, ground ginger, dried or baker's yeast, granulated sugar.

2 Get permission to start, wash your hands, and sterilize all your equipment.

3 Pour five quarts of warm boiled water into one of the buckets and stir in one pound of sugar until it dissolves.

4 Mix one ounce of cream of tartar and one ounce of ground ginger with a little water in a pitcher, stirring all the time.

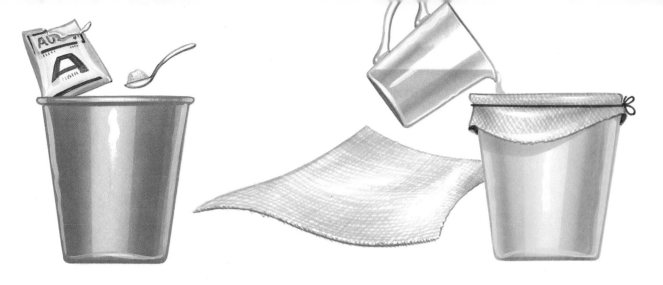

5 Add the mixture to the bucket of water, and stir thoroughly.

6 Add one heaping teaspoon of yeast to the bucket, and stir again.

7 Tie the cheesecloth over the top of the second bucket, and pour the liquid from the first bucket through the cheesecloth to strain it.

8 Using the funnel, fill the bottles with the strained liquid from the second bucket.

9 Screw the caps on the bottles, and leave them overnight – or longer – in a warm place.

10 Next day, taste the fruits of your labors. Open a bottle carefully, and pour yourself some ginger ale.

Trees

Trees are the largest of all plants. Their trunks grow about an inch each year, so you can tell how old they are by measuring the girth of their trunks. Measure the girth by putting a tape measure around the trunk about five feet from the ground. The measurement will tell you roughly how old the tree is.

If you find a tree that has been cut down, you can tell its age precisely. Inside any tree, there is a ring of tubes that carry water from the roots to the leaves. The ring grows every year and forms a new ring of wood.

There are two kinds of rings – narrow ones and wide ones. The narrow ones are dark. They show the layer of wood produced in the autumn when growth was slow. The wide ones show the fast growth of spring and summer.

The width of the rings varies from year to year. This is usually because of the weather. A thin summer ring might mean that there was a drought, a thick one that the summer was hot and wet. Find a tree stump, and work out the tree's age and what the weather was like when you were growing up.

To make rubbings of trees, use crayons on the bark and pencils on the leaves. Make prints of the leaves with shoe polish or thick paint.

New Plants From Old

You do not always need seeds or spores to grow new plants. Strawberry plants spread themselves with slender stems called runners that travel along the ground. African violets will grow buds and roots if you make small cuts in their leaves. Potatoes, which are swollen stems, grow from their "eyes," which are buds. Tulips grow from bulbs which store the plant's food.

Some plants grow from cuttings. Cut a woody stem from a rose, and push it deep into the soil. It should grow roots and start to sprout. You can buy rooting powder to give it a good start.

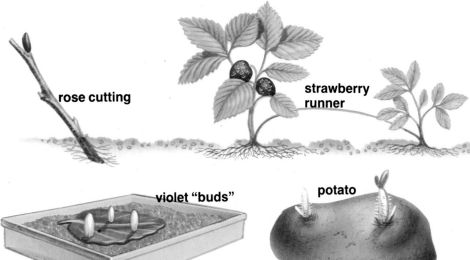

rose cutting

strawberry runner

violet "buds"

potato

tulip bulb

You can use cuttings from small plants to make a bottle garden.

A Bottle Garden

1 You need a large glass jar or bottle with a top, some pretty pebbles or stones, pieces of wood or bark, some potting soil, and cuttings or seedlings of moss, ferns, ivy, and other small plants.

2 Put a layer of soil in the jar, arrange the pebbles and wood, and plant the plants firmly in between them.

3 When you have an attractive arrangement, water your garden, but do not swamp it. From now on, it will need little attention. The plants will drink the water and release it into the air. Because it is in a bottle, the moisture will not disappear. It will condense on the glass and trickle back into the soil.

4 Keep your garden in a light, but not too sunny, spot indoors – and enjoy it!

Index and Glossary